CW00410924

Toxic Relationship and Anxiety in Relationship

Take the reins of your relationship and learn from this empath survival guide. Find out how to handle a narcissist.

Tim Spider

Table of Contents

CHAPTER 8: EXPLORING SOME OF THE LIFESTYLES AND MYTHS OF NPD 12

    Is a little bit of narcissism healthy? 13

    Loving without self-love 15

    NPD and How It Shows Up In the Workplace 19

    Narcissism and Workaholics 25

CHAPTER 9: HOW TO ASK FOR HELP WHEN DEALING WITH A NARCISSIST 32

    When should I ask for help? 34

    Taking those first steps 36

    A case study of the demoralized woman 39

    Whom should you ask for help? 42

    How to deal with the varied reactions 45

    How can I help someone with NPD? 47

    How to help yourself 51

CHAPTER 10: UNDERSTANDING MEGALOMANIA 55

    The role that low self-esteem has to play 57

    Shame issues and NPD 61

    Covering for weaknesses vs. real strength 64

    Kohut's Model 67

    Cultural considerations 70

CHAPTER 11: NARCISSISM AND DEPRESSION 76

THE DEPRESSIVE NARCISSISTS 77

DEALING WITH NEEDS THAT ARE NOT MET 82

DEPRESSION AS THE OPPOSITE OF ADORATION 84

LOSING THE NARCISSISTIC SUPPLY 88

**CHAPTER 12: HOW TO HANDLE YOUR INTERACTIONS
WITH A NARCISSIST 94**

HOW CAN I TALK TO SOMEONE WHO HAS NPD? 98

HOW CAN I STAY STRONG AND NOT LET THE NARCISSIST MANIPULATE ME?
.... 103

CAN I GET WHAT I WANT FROM A NARCISSIST? 107

HOW TO STOP BEING VICTIMIZED OR ABUSED BY THE NARCISSIST 110

CONCLUSION 117

Furthermore, the transmission, duplication, or reproduction of any of the following work including specific information will be considered an illegal act irrespective of if it is done electronically or in print. This extends to creating a secondary or tertiary copy of the work or a recorded copy and is only allowed with the express written consent from the Publisher. All additional right reserved.

The information in the following pages is broadly considered a truthful and accurate account of facts and as such, any inattention, use, or misuse of the information in question by the reader will render any resulting actions solely under their purview. There are no scenarios in which the publisher or the original author of this work can be in any fashion deemed liable for any hardship or damages that may befall them after undertaking information described herein.

Additionally, the information in the following pages is intended only for informational purposes and should thus be thought of as universal. As befitting its nature, it is presented without assurance regarding its prolonged validity or interim quality. Trademarks that are mentioned are done without written consent and can in no way be considered an endorsement from the trademark holder.

Chapter 1: Exploring Some of the Lifestyles and Myths of NPD

As most people enter the world of being an adult, they are going to find reality, accept the person they are, and deal with the ups and downs that come in life by being the best that they can. But then there are some of those who find that it is hard to live a lifestyle that is normal. They want to keep being that superhero they were as a child, and they are not able to understand why things need to change. In this chapter, we are going to take a look at some of the myths and lifestyles of someone who has narcissism and why it is so important to understand what is real and what isn't.

Is a little bit of narcissism healthy?

The way that we use the word narcissism in our modern world means that the answer to whether narcissism is healthy or not can go either way. It has its good side and its bad side. A healthy amount of narcissism is often seen as a good thing, like having an attitude that is confident.

 It's in people who know themselves, who are able to accept both their weaknesses and their strengths, and who have a sense of what is good and bad about them.

When there is a healthy amount of narcissism in the individual, it is going to include a level of self-love that makes the person want to look and do their best, while still balancing some appreciation, care, and love for others. Everyone is going to have a few traits that are narcissistic. It is part of both your early development as a child and your adult life. This is because we all have wants and needs, and there are going to be times when these show up more than others.

If you have a healthy amount of narcissism, and you use it to better yourself while still showing some compassion to those around you, then yes, a bit of narcissism is healthy in your life. It allows you to not get stepped on and put down by others all the time. And it makes it easier to know your own worth no matter who you are around.

Loving without self-love

Love is a very interesting topic and one that a lot of people do not fully understand for themselves yet. Whether we are talking about love for others or self-love, it is something that people throughout the years are going to try their hardest to explain, even though they may come up short.

However, it is important to remember here that when it comes to self-love, you shouldn't confuse loving yourself (which all of us need to do on occasion), with unhealthy narcissism. In fact, many therapists have worked with those who have narcissism and NPD as those who don't have a lot of self-love. This is because when they take a look at themselves in the mirror, all they see is an image, rather than something that is true. Self-love is going to be loving yourself the way you are now and not the way you imagine yourself in your head. Self-love is going to be healthy, rather than selfish, and that is what distinguishes it from narcissistic tendencies.

In the Zen ideology, the idea of loving oneself is going to be all about the total dedication towards becomes a better person, about not needing to always be the top priority in each group, and about making sure that your emotional, mental, and physical health are all in line. With these ideas, a person is going to need to be available to put the needs of others first, to empathize with others, and to care about others.

While this does allow some room for you to stop and take care of yourself on occasion, it also recognizes that you need to be open and willing to take care of those around you as well. There are some theorists who will propose how self-love is going to be a more peaceful state of mind, one where challenges are not able to bother you because you have earned how to be safe and balanced. This can do wonders when it comes to your inner strengths, and it will allow your abilities to shine out.

It is important for you to love yourself because once you are able to do that, it is possible to love others. There arc many schools of thought that will talk about how important it is to be connected with those around you and to work on serving these individuals. And doing this is going to be hard if you don't have self-love for yourself. This is where a lot of narcissists are going to run into trouble. They don't realize that the image they love about themselves is a false one, and so they have no self-love. Since they don't love themselves, it is almost impossible for them to love or care about, or even help, those around them.

NPD and How It Shows Up In the Workplace

This brings up an interesting point about how well the narcissist is able to perform in the workplace. They don't get along with others, and they constantly need to be the center of attention in order to feel good. This can seem to make it difficult for them to get along with others and do well at work. But everywhere we look, even at work, there are going to be narcissist around as well.

There has been some recent research that shows that narcissists have what it takes to be leaders. This is because, even though they may use people and not get along with others, they have a lot of leadership characteristics like competitiveness, assertiveness, energy, and motivation. However, just because they have these characteristics doesn't mean that they are going to be successful, and it is possible that, whether or not they become successful, they could cause some problems for those who work there, and for the business as a whole.

One issue that comes up here is that the narcissist is not going to like a compromise, admitting that they are the one who did the error or failure. And all of these things are going to be natural parts of doing business and of working. Not accepting them can cause some issues about this.

While there are a lot of narcissists in the world around us, it is important to know that there is a downside. Yes, they can bring some great traits to leadership and they can be really good at their job if they are interested in doing it well, but often, these people are going to be the ones who cause problems in the business, and it is even worse because the narcissist doesn't see that they are the one who caused the damage. They may choose to distort the issue or deny that they had anything to do with it. These narcissists are going to work to justify themselves or they will make a lot of rationalizations that will help to make their own self-worth go up but won't do any good for anyone else.

This is why many companies need to be careful about who they are working with. There are some narcissists who are able to rein it in a bit and can keep doing an amazing job as managers. But if the narcissist is not able to control themselves, and they run into trouble accepting things, or admitting that they are wrong, it is possible that the narcissistic leader will end up taking the company and leading it to the ground.

Remember that these narcissists are not going to be that fond of learning from others. They like to be the ones who dominate, the ones who make speeches, and they are not likely to listen to others. Even though they like to be surrounded by a big group of women and men who agree with everything they say, the narcissist has no true want to do teamwork.

Working with a boss who is a narcissist is going to be difficult. They are going to be demanding, will not listen to your requests or concerns at all, no matter how valid these are, and they can make your workspace really hard to deal with. Some of the tips that you can keep in mind in order to avoid some of the potential problems with a narcissistic boss include:

1. Try to keep some good records of the work that you do. This helps you in case any narcissistic managers or coworkers start to misinterpret your intentions. It also keeps them from taking credit for the accomplishments and work that you are doing.

2. Keep all of the communication you do with them professional. It is sometimes tempting to confide in the narcissist, but if you do that, be prepared for them to take your words and use them to their own advantage if they need.

3. It can be hard to deal with this kind of boss. But remember that the issues have nothing to do with you, and are more about the narcissism.

4. If you feel that your boss is making a decision that is really bad, you can still give your opinion. But the best way to do this is to show them your alternative and then discuss how the narcissist is personally going to be able to benefit from this change.

5. Make sure that they know your personal boundaries and that you expect them to stick with these.

Narcissism and Workaholics

Since it is now more common than ever to find narcissism in the workplace, it seems more likely that there is a link between the narcissistic personality traits and those who are typically called workaholics. Hard work is a good thing, just like having self-confidence can be a good thing. But when either of these is blown out of proportion too much, it is going to end up harming others. And when work is carried to the point where it excludes all else, it is going to be workaholism and it can be harmful to the narcissist and everyone who is related or near the.

There is no denying that the people of America are hardworking people. And it seems that in our current economy and with wages staying pretty stagnant, people are working more now than ever. It isn't uncommon to find people working two or three jobs in the hopes of making ends meet. But there is a difference between working hard to get by or because you love your job and the issues of workaholism.

When we are looking at the workaholic, it seems like everything and anything is going to come behind the work, even family. Vacation and social engagements are not going to be a part of their life. And they will basically become their job, not allowing anything else to come in. And often, this is going to come with narcissism because the workaholic is able to define their sense of self with the job. To the workaholic, the job is going to be a false image of who they are, and it is so important to them because it allows them to escape from reality, just like the false sense of the narcissist does.

With so many similarities that are showing up between the personalities of a workaholic and a narcissist, it is no wonder that *Psychology Today* recently published a study that found that those who are admitted workaholics are going to score highly on a personality scale that measures obsessive perfectionism and narcissism.

Want to see how close these two personality traits are to each other? We have already gone through and talked about some of the personality traits that come with being a narcissist, now let's explore some of the traits that you are going to see with a workaholic. When we are looking at a workaholic, we are looking at a person who:

1. Pursues power and values self-importance to help support a grandiose image of their self-worth and to get more admiration from those they work with.

2. Overproduce in order to make themselves be above, or at least seem superior, to those they work with.

3. They let work become almost an obsession, in a similar manner that a narcissist works to fill their narcissistic supply. These people are only able to find the value in themselves through their work.

4. These people are going to see some expectations of themselves that are unrealistic. They expect that their performance needs to be perfect.

5. They are very impatient about getting to the next level.

6. They are compulsive.

7. They are really into using busyness as a defense to escape from some of the emotional commitments that they have or some of the negative emotions that they need to work with.

When we get down to the roots of both problems, we see that workaholism and narcissism are both going to be conditions that result from either a poorly defined sense of self or one that is false. Being able to develop this healthy sense of self is going to require a feeling of identity and of being worthwhile, and it needs to develop separately from either the failures or the accomplishments of the individual. But while this may be something that most people are able to work with, it is something that both workaholics and narcissists struggle with.

As you can see, working with a narcissist and understanding how this whole process works is something that is going to take some time and effort in order to accomplish. These people can often take over as a leader, and since they don't have empathy for others, it is sometimes difficult to work with them. Knowing how to look out for this personality type and working to protect yourself can make working in that situation easier over time.

Chapter 2: How to Ask for Help When Dealing with a Narcissist

When you are on the receiving end of narcissism, it is hard to figure out what to do. You need to know that it is perfectly fine and okay for you to take a step back from this relationship, no matter who they are and take care of yourself. You need to know what to do and how to do something for yourself so that you can start to feel good as well.

Of course, asking for help can sometimes be difficult to do in these situations. Often when you need this help with a narcissist, it is because you have been with them for a long time, or you are in what you thought was an intimate relationship with them. This can make you feel like you did something wrong like you are too weak, or like others are going to make fun of you. But it is nearly impossible to be with a narcissist and to handle it on your own without some help.

Asking for help is not a sign of weakness. It is a sign that you are ready to start taking care of yourself and you are ready to stop putting the narcissist first. When you are ready to start reaching out for help, who are you going to reach out to? And what kind of help is there for you when you want to deal with this narcissist? Let's take a look at some of the options that are available to you, and what you can do when you are ready to change the relationship and you need help dealing with a narcissist.

When should I ask for help?

As soon as you notice that you are dealing with a narcissist, it is time to get the help that you need. Don't feel bad if you have been in the relationship for some time. Narcissists know that if they come on too strong in the beginning, they will scare others away from them. If no one will be around the narcissist, then the narcissist will not be able to get their fill of attention and love from that chosen person.

Because of this, the narcissist is often going to be able to trick you into not realizing what is going on. They will seem like they are loving, that they are a sweet talker, and like they are the one for you. By the time most people figure out that they are dealing with this narcissist, they have been together or in some kind of relationship for a long time.

Don't let this stop you from getting the help that you need. Yes, it may seem like you are making things up. And maybe you worry that feeling this way means that you were dumb and missed out on the signs. In reality, you probably did miss out on some signs, but the narcissist is really good at hiding themselves and making sure that you can't see these signs until it is too late.

So, it is best if you are able to take a stand and ask for help as soon as you realize that you are dealing with a narcissist. Even if it is hard. Even if it feels like you are going to look like a fool and that others are going to make fun of you. Even if you worry that you are seeing things or making things up in your head. If you start to suspect that you are dealing with a narcissist, then it is likely that you truly are, and you need to get the help that you can as early as possible.

Taking those first steps

There are a lot of men and women who will go through the same experience of dealing with narcissism. Maybe they knew a child, a friend, a parent, a sibling, a lover, a spouse or someone else who seemed to have the real problem with narcissism. It is something that all of us have heard about. It seems that with our current culture and the media that is around us, it is easier than ever to hear about and meet up with narcissists of all kind.

Because of the media and other things that go on around us, we may wonder if we are actually dealing with someone who is a narcissist, or if we are just blowing the picture up too big in our heads.

One good way to check is to see how the person responds when you try to talk through it with them. Maybe if you go and talk about how it feels like you haven't been able to see your friends in some time. If they agree and then suggest you should set up a girl's night out or something similar, then it's likely that life has just gotten in the way, and that is why you haven't had time to go out with friends.

But, when you are dealing with a narcissist, they don't want you to have any connections, outside of the connection that you have with them. They want you to just take care of them, so suggesting that you go out with some friends and family would be a foreign idea to them. They may get defensive about it, try to tell you that it is a bad idea, and will try to do everything in their power to not let you go, while still making it look like it was your idea.

If you are pretty sure that you are dealing with someone who is a narcissist, then it is time to get some help. Of course, it is not always hard to think about getting help to feel okay, but this is a good thing to do. Many of those who figure out that they are in a relationship with someone who is a narcissist may feel ashamed to ask anyone else for help and they may think, wrongly of course, that they were not smart enough or have enough resilience in order to do the work themselves.

The first step is to realize that you are dealing with someone who is a narcissist. Since the narcissist is often going to do what is in their power to ensure you don't realize this fact because this means that they lose out on their supply, just getting with this breakthrough is going to make a big difference in your own overall health and well-being. Once you realize this, you will be able to take the next step in looking for the right help, both for you and for the person who suffers from narcissism.

A case study of the demoralized woman

Let's look at an example of what can happen in a narcissistic relationship. One young woman, who is typical of many others regardless of their gender, had written online about how she had to ask for help in order to help herself and others who may have been in a similar situation as her. After being in a relationship for five years with a man she had thought was her dream man, she found that her world ended up collapsing around her. She found that it was hard to cope.

It had actually been an escalating nightmare for those five years. She talked about how she felt so alone and lost in that relationship, not really understanding how things happened, or why they ended up happening. Because of the boyfriend's constant demoralizing and berating, she believed that all the things wrong and all of the things that didn't go right in that relationship were her fault. Yet, even with this going on, she still wanted to keep this man in her life, though he had gone on and found another girlfriend.

Over time, while she was dealing with this and still trying to figure out how to get the man she loved back, she revealed some of the situations to one of her friends. At the time, the friend suggested that she go and see her own therapist. After doing an evaluation, the therapist told this woman that her boyfriend was a narcissist. The woman had to then figure out how to accept this truth. This man, who was most likely a narcissist, could not feel compassion, empathy, or love for her.

With some therapy and some time, this woman reached a point where she was able to realize that this man, no matter how much she had loved him, had been able to deplete all of your mental, emotional, and physical energy, and then he was able to leave when there was no more left to give. This is when she realized that it was time to ask for help.

Whom should you ask for help?

The story above is similar to what a lot of women, and sometimes even men, will experience when they get in a relationship with a narcissist. They are led to believe that they are worthless and that all of the problems that come up in the relationship are their own fault. They are told that they are worthless and that they are not perfect. And yet, they cling to that person, loving them through it all. Once the narcissist is able to take everything they can from the victim, they leave, without feeling any remorse or anything else.

Going through this situation can leave you feeling a bit embarrassed, and you may find it hard to talk to those around you. But, if you do have a potential narcissist or a narcissist in your life, then all health professionals agree that you need to have at least two people on your side as support. These include a family member and a trustworthy friend who will listen to your feelings, listen to your fears, and help with the pain. You should also consider working with a professional who will be able to answer any of the questions that you have at this time, and who will be able to give you an objective way to deal with the situation.

If you are not able to find a close friend or family member to work with, don't let this stop you from getting the help that you need. If you have been dealing with a narcissist, you are probably feeling lost and alone. And if you have been in a relationship with one for a longer period of time, then you may have alienated a lot of your friends and family and have no one to turn to. Don't let this keep you back from getting the help that you need.

Finding a professional to help you, even if you are not able to get the narcissist to get treatment too, will do a ton of good. They will be able to discuss if your partner really was a narcissist, what all of this means, and can help you to handle the situation in a way that will guide you to your own self-esteem and self-worth coming back. This can help you deal and get your life back on track after all of the things that the narcissist was able to take from you.

How to deal with the varied reactions

Of course, we all know those people who are quick to judge others, and usually, they are willing to do this in a negative, rather than a positive, manner.

And that can happen when you decide to become open about the narcissist in your life. Even when you do it to some of the people you are closest to in your life, they may not understand the situation or the decisions that you make for yourself and your children as this situation gets worse. This is even harder to do if the narcissist had met some of these people and made a great outward appearance to them.

Depending on your own family, telling them about being with a potential narcissist will not get you the response that you are looking for. They may say things like "All men are dogs" "Just give him time" or even "You have to be joking, no way, he's so charming and special". This can happen with your friends as well. And many times, this happens because the narcissist has done such a good job of deceiving those around them.

This can be hard to deal with. You want to get some help and support, but others are just not seeing the damn thing that you are. They assume that you are seeing it the wrong way, or that you are just lying to get them to go against the narcissist. And when others are unfair to you or choose not to listen to what you are saying, it can make the situation even harder to deal with

How can I help someone with NPD?

Caring about and wanting to help the narcissist means that you are already coming to this situation with goodness and concern. As for the narcissist, what can be done for them is always at the forefront of their lives. So, one important thing that you can do here is to take a step back, find out how you can detach, and then use the empathy that you have in life in order to understand and try to be helpful.

While there are many therapists who believe that a narcissist is able to change for the better, it is something that takes a lot of work.

It is possible for you to get the whole thing off to a good start, but it is usually going to be some sort of mental health professional who will be able to help the narcissist. Seeing a therapist for yourself can make it easier to handle the problems as well. Depending on the situation and how willing the narcissist is to doing the work, you may see a therapist on your own, the therapist may work with you and the narcissist separately, or you and the narcissist may do some therapy together.

Some of the best things that you can do to help you get started with getting them the help that they need, and to ensure that you really know what is going on here, include:

1. Ask your partner, the one with NPD, to write down what they expect from you, and any of the places where they think you are falling short. Consider any of the points that are reasonable and then ignore the rest. Inform your partner about what you think is on the list that is

unreasonable and explain why. Let them know that this is not up for argument or discussion.

2. To help the person with NPD to choose to go to some kind of counseling, whether it is marriage or single counseling, you can tell them that you need them to help bring the relationship back to the intimacy, love, and warmth that it used to have.

3. Admit that there are some faults of your own that you would like to get fixed so that you can be a better spouse. This helps them to see that counseling is not just all about them, so they are more willing to go. Of course, this is not a place where the narcissist is allowed to take that admission and rattle off a long list of your shortcomings. Be firm in this. If the narcissist starts doing that, then tell them the conversation is over and walk away.

4. You can sometimes appeal to the narcissism that is there by humoring your partner until you are able to get some better advice from a

professional so you know the best way to proceed.

Another thing to consider here is that you probably shouldn't go home and then proclaim that your pattern is a narcissist. This is going to put anyone on the defensive, whether they are a narcissist or not, and can cause a lot more problems than it is going to solve. Instead, you can try to make some changes in your lifestyle. For example, if they try to interrupt you when you are talking, stop and say something like "I was finishing my story. Please let me continue. It hurts my feelings when you interrupt because it makes me feel like you don't value what I have to say." This works nicely because it lets you call out the behavior that is bothering you, gives a small goal for the narcissist to focus on and makes sure that you are able to concentrate on your feelings as well.

How to help yourself

Along with this idea is the fact that you need to take care of yourself. You have spent some time working on making the narcissist happy, making sure that their needs are met.

And it is likely that you have gone for some time without having any of your needs met or your feelings listened to in some time. During this time, it is important that you stop and learn how you can take care of yourself as well. Some of the things that you can do if you find that this relationship has done a number on your self-esteem include:

1. Spend time with those who think highly of you.
2. Do some activities that you find enjoyable, ones that make you feel great.
3. Do something that is good for yourself.
4. Join up for some kind of community or service group. You can even consider signing up for school or just a few classes.

5. Develop some new hobbies and take the time to actually do them.

6. Work on expanding out your circle of friends. You want to make sure that these are friends that are separate from the narcissist, ones that are healthy and good for you.

7. Try to make up your own support group, one that has at least three healthy adults. This helps you to get some new points of view and will make sure that you learn the differences between healthy behaviors and unhealthy ones.

If you can get the narcissist to agree to help, then this is great news. But in many cases, you are going to be the one who will go for help, and this is fine, too. You have been through a big experience, and taking the time to come out of that and to realize your own self-worth is going to be just as important as anything else.

Chapter 3: Understanding Megalomania

The next topic that we are going to take a look at is known as megalomania. Sometimes, you may find that living with someone who has NPD is going to be like living with a maniac. And this does make a bit of sense because narcissism used to go by a different name, megalomania. This term basically means power mad.

Not everyone who is a narcissist or who has NPD is going to be dealing with the megalomania. This term is usually reserved for those who are in one of the most destructive and most extreme forms of NPD. The megalomaniac is going to have a need for absolute control and total power of those they are around. This means that when they are around another person, they are going to want to be in control over how that victim talks, walks, dresses, and thinks.

If you are reading through this, and you are worried that this is the exact situation that you yourself are dealing with, know that you are not alone in this. In fact, narcissism is often one of the few pathological conditions that are going to cause more pain and duress not to its sufferers, but to those who are closest to the one with NPD.

The role that low self-esteem has to play

When you hear about the word megalomania, it is likely to bring up an image of someone who is pretentious, egotistical, and conceited, and other signals that are going to be useful when you want to describe a narcissist. But under all of this self-importance and arrogance is going to be like a self-esteem that is very fragile and may not even exist all that much. That is why, even with all of the noise and the bravado, those who are dealing with narcissism are going to struggle when it comes to even minor amounts of criticism.

When working with megalomania, despite what we may assume, you may find someone who, on the inside, is easily going to feel humiliated or ashamed.

And when they feel this way on the inside, they are going to try and make themselves feel better, usually by going into a rage. They may decide that there is a need for them to belittle others in order to make up for the things that are missing or lacking in themselves.

Many psychologists are going to agree that while most narcissists are going to believe in that false image that they show the world, they do not feel that what makes up this image is going to be enough for them to really be better or superior to those around them. If they did, they would not need to constantly be around others, or constantly be looking for praise, in order to feel better.

There are times when a person who is suffering from NPD will show their true selves and they may reveal this low self-image to some. But when this happens, they are going to do it in a way to get compliments to feed their egos and to help them feel better. In one online forum, a husband is going to talk about this situation with a wife who had NPD. In this situation, he talked about how his wife would say negative things about herself and be self-deprecating. But over time, he started to see that it was all an act. All that this wife wanted was for her husband to constantly tell her how wonderful she was. Then, when he started to realize what was going on, he stopped giving the compliments.

Whether a narcissist is going to have low self-esteem or high self-esteem has been very controversial over the years. There are a lot of researchers believe that the push for high self-esteem, which a lot of self-help gurus and motivational speakers are going to push hard, and the praise that is heaped on a lot of young people to encourage them, could be a major reason that the cases of narcissism have risen. Whether it is because of this or because of low self-esteem that more narcissists tend to be showing up throughout the world is something that will need to be studied more in depth.

Shame issues and NPD

Some researchers think that this narcissism is going to be a kind of defense that the individual can put up in order to protect themselves against shame.

The narcissist may use shame in order to take that image they have made of their true self and protect them. It is a defense that is going to cause them a fight-or-flight response in those who are suffering from NPD, meaning that the individual will either run away or they will lash out.

Guilt can often cause a more personal response, such as asking the other person to forgive them or coming clean about the thing that they did wrong. But when it comes to shaming, this is going to come much more easily to the narcissist than that of guilt. It is possible for the narcissist to feel ashamed about the actions that they did, but will usually not admit that they have done something wrong.

Shame is going to be an emotional response to being imperfect or flawed. Many believe that it is tied into underlying low **self-esteem**, something that is found in some of the other problems that are tied to narcissism as well. While shame will have more to do with how the person feels about themselves, it can also be tied to what others think and how they are going to judge you. If a person believes that others see them as inferior, making a lot of mistakes, or lacking, it can lead to them feeling some shame

When we are talking about narcissism, this is going to be known as the grandiosity gap. This is going to be the difference between the information that the person with NPD gets from the real world and their false self-image. The greater the contrast between these two, the greater the gap and the greater the feelings of shame.

Many times, the narcissist wants to feel like they are separated from others by either being better than them or above them. But then they reach a conflict because they are seen as different from others and they have a fear of this. This is more of a feeling of otherness that they have to deal with. Narcissists are going to feel ashamed of their flaws, and any imperfections that make them different from other people. And this can cause even more problems than before.

Covering for weaknesses vs. real strength

Outwardly, the narcissists, especially if they are described by therapists as megalomaniacs, are going to appear to the outside world as confident, powerful, and strong. But when you really dig down deep and learn more about them, you will find that the opposite is true. What appears to be strength on the outside is simply, in the case of a megalomaniac, covering up for some of the weaknesses that are on the inside.

In fact, one way to distinguish healthy narcissism from unhealthy narcissism is the fact that the former is going to recognize their own strengths while still accepting the weaknesses. But someone with NPD is not going to even have the ability to look and see that they are made up of traits that are both bad and good. They see anything that may be a bit negative about themselves as a weakness, and so, they will try to hide it, and overcompensate so that this negative won't show up in their image.

Many narcissists, but specifically those who are megalomaniacs, are going to see that the world is in absolutes, with no area for greys in there. They, and everything else that is found in their world will either be all good or all bad, and there is no in between with this. When we take a look into their minds, we see that they want to be all powerful, and this is impossible if they have any weaknesses at all.

Unlike the typical narcissist, people who accept that they can have strength, along with some weaknesses, understand that they don't need to be the best or the most powerful at everything in order to be successful. This is how normal people are going to view the world. It doesn't mean that we really like the weaknesses that we have, but that we are willing to accept them. With a narcissist, they turn this around and just overcompensate or say that they don't have any weaknesses at all.

Kohut's Model

One of the leading theorists of narcissism that we need to take a look at here is going to be Heinz Kohut. His work is the basic foundation of treating and understanding narcissism.

All humans are going to share the experience as children where they have a grandiose self-image and they idealize parents as the caregivers who are willing to give in and cater to all the needs of the child. With this in mind, Kohut was the first to suggest that narcissism could be a stunted form of development as we enter into adulthood.

In his writing, Kohut explains that as most children develop, they start to see more of the reality of the world, and their grand illusions are going to be replaced so that they can mature. When someone goes through a healthy development, the illusions of grandiosity that they had in the past are going to slowly move over as they gain more self-esteem. But if something happens, often some kind of emotional trauma, this primitive image of the self is going to stay intact and it won't change. And this is what happens in narcissistic personality disorder.

To look a bit more at his work, Kohut would describe a person with NPD as quick to anger, edgy, and irritable. The rage that would often show up in a narcissist would be the result of narcissistic wounds that occurred to that false image we talked about before. Kohut went on to say that the key to overcoming this disorder was to teach this person what empathy is all about.

This is the main goal of all good therapies for treating NPD. Once the narcissist is able to empathize with others, they are going to be able to handle dealing with their self-esteem and fixing some of the other issues that may come up.

Cultural considerations

While this disorder is not just found in the United States, many people think that the foundations as well as the modern values of modern America are more likely to promote this narcissism.

The main stressors that are common in our modern society are going to include things like isolation, loneliness, and alienation. And then, to make the matter worse, our culture is going to teach us that it is best to withdraw when we are confronted with a situation that is stressful. Because of this, it is no surprise that narcissism is so common in the United States, and with other countries who value individualism.

It is possible that people in other countries are going to develop this disorder as well. But the modern society in America and the things that a lot of the people in this society value can make narcissism turn into an epidemic. There are a lot of reasons for this. It could be because people value being isolated and alone. And it could be because many parents are being overindulgent, providing a huge reward on accomplishments, even if they are minor. This may seem like good parenting, but it can make children feel like they are super special and that they should always get recognition for their accomplishments, no matter how big or small.

Another thing that could be causing the rise in narcissism is that there is no longer the value in our culture, as there was in the past, that pridefulness is a sin. There are pastors out there now who will preach that God wants us to be rich. There are sports celebrities who say that selfishness is actually a virtue. There is this pride in everything, and it is causing some issues all around.

To add to this is the fact that many people find that they work and live as separate individuals, apart from others and even freelancing because of the use of technology. There are a ton of advantages to being able to telecommute, such as more job opportunities, spending more time with your family, and more, but if you spend all day only interacting with a piece of technology could mean that we start to lose some of our humanity.

Since working alone means that you do not need to rely on others as much, and you don't need to show consideration to keep the peace at work, and you don't need to make compromises, it is easier to fall into some of the tendencies of narcissism.

It is important to note that people who have NPD can be driven by shame and fears. They are fearful of being made fun of, of others abandoning them, and to appear that they are lacking or that they have weaknesses of any kInd. The increased amount of isolation socially in our digital era is going to increase this issue and can mean that more and more people are going to deal with narcissism over time. It can also end up taking them out of an environment in which they may see that their negative behavior is actually impacting others.

While living in this kind of world doesn't mean that you are automatically going to become a narcissist, it can increase the risk, and it means that more and more people are dealing with this issue. As there is a rise in narcissistic behavior of a world where the people only care about their own wants or needs without having any care of empathy of what others are going through, it may be time to make some changes before it gets out of hand.

Chapter 4: Narcissism and Depression

After spending some time reading through this guidebook and learning more about narcissism, it can be really hard for you to feel any sorrow for them. And if you have been on the other side of this illness and seen how it can affect you, you are less likely to have any worries about their feelings. Narcissists are often going to come across to others as boastful, proud, and full of themselves. And because of this, it is really hard to see that there is a lot of self-confidence, self-esteem, and even depression issues underneath.

However, many of those who are narcissists are going to deal with a variety of other issues including depression. We are going to spend some time in this chapter taking a look at the link between narcissism and depression and how this is going to affect the sufferer.

The depressive narcissists

When a narcissist enters into treatment, it is rare that they think that they are dealing with the narcissism. It is usually some other side effect, such as anxiety or depression, that will get them to go and seek help from a counselor.

Of course, as we have described in this guidebook, there are a number of side effects that are going to come with narcissism, such as depression, eating disorders, and addition, and it is likely that the narcissist is going to enter into treatment because of one of these.

While those who have NPD often will not show a lot of the typical signs that come with mental illness, it is common for them to notice they are suffering some of the symptoms of depression, and they will seek help for this. Depression here is going to be linked to a term that is known as narcissistic wounds.

Many times, narcissists are going to feel depressed when they feel that they are losing or failure. They are going to come to a therapist or other counselor complaining that they feel empty, or that they are going to be bored easily when they aren't able to stimulate themselves on a higher level. Depression that shows up in a narcissist is going to be the result of repeated failures, whether these actually happened or they were imagined by the narcissist.

Usually, when you encounter a depressive narcissist, you will find that they are going to be big perfectionists. When life ends up not going like bland, which is what will happen at some point, depressive narcissists are more likely to blame themselves, and they can sometimes be overtaken with shame, something that leads them into even more depression than before.

If life with a narcissist is tough, then living with a depressed narcissist is going to seem like it is possible. Once they reach this state of depression, they may decide that it is time to turn everyone and everything around them into something that is negative. Their sense of melancholy can get so strong that everything the narcissist experiences can make them go into a deeper depression. This is a big swing, going from one side (being happy and joyful) to the other side (being down and depressed about everything).

When a narcissist starts to get depressed, it is possible that they may cry randomly, where before they would refuse to show emotions of any kind. Don't let this fool you though. Often, these tears are going to be crocodile tears so that they are able to get some sympathy and attention to substitute for that supply they are losing when it comes to attention.

It is during this stage where some other self-destructive behaviors like suicide attempts and self-mutilation could start showing up. But many times, these are going to be half-hearted. The narcissist doesn't really want to harm themselves or even kill themselves. Instead, they want to get attention to the action. If they are able to gain some sympathy and some attention out of the situation, then they see themselves as successful.

The biggest problem that can come up here is that for the most time, nothing that you try to do or say is going to snap the depressive narcissist out of their depression. This just turns into an additional defense mechanism that the narcissist is going to start relying on. This is a new persona that the narcissist is going to start relying on and anything that you try to do or say is going to be turned around, ensuring that it fits the worldview that the depressed narcissist has.

Dealing with needs that are not met

Most of us realize that we are not always able to get what we want. But a true narcissist is going to have a lot of trouble dealing with this kind of advice, and they often won't decide to take that advice.

Despite what they think, those who have NPD are not always going to get what they want. This is often because they have expectations that are so high that they will never be able to get the thing that they need. And when they aren't able to get what they want; you end up with a narcissist who is going to cause a lot of trouble. If you are around this person, there are going to be violent temper tantrums and angry outbursts. And the narcissist is going to find that they end up with some form of depression as well.

Many of those who are around a narcissist feel like they are near a volcano that is about to explode. And often, the depression that comes out of this is going to be a reaction to these pockets of aggression that is buried down deep, but they refuse to acknowledge that there is anything going on. Depression in a narcissist is going to be a bit different than what you will see with others because it is more of aggression bottled up and then turned inward.

Depression as the opposite of adoration

The main goal of most narcissists is to be adored and to have others idolize them. And if the narcissist could get others to worship them, then they would be even happier. But what would happen if this is not the case? You may think about the image of an aging screen star or a movie star who lost their beauty, their fame and fans, and then they retreat into themselves, crying over the past. This could be a good way to describe what the NPD person is going to feel when they stop getting some of the adoration that they need.

It is in the nature of humans to admire people, and it is common that you are going to put another person on a pedestal. They may do this with a celebrity, a coworker, relative, or a friend. What happens with this though is that the person who is placed on the pedestal may not have the abilities to hold up to the expectations that you have of this. And then, when you end up seeing that person for who they really are, they may not seem like they are as admirable as you had thought.

But this is going to turn into a horrible problem that you are going to need to deal with when the person you put on the pedestal happens to be a narcissist, and you live with them. When you met the narcissist in the beginning, it may be easy to place them on the pedestal. Many narcissists know how to be sexy, successful, charismatic, charming, and more in order to get you to pay attention and put your focus on them. This allows them to get put right on the pedestal where they want to be.

But, over time, and the more time you spend with them, you will find that the truth will start to come out, and you see that the narcissist doesn't really belong on that pedestal. When you decide to take them down, you are going to end up with some devastating effects, not only on the narcissist but also with yourself.

In any relationship, you may think that you have found the perfect partner to work with. And when you are in the beginning, it is likely that you are going to create an ideal version of the partner. You may know that there are some bad things, but you choose to just focus on the good. This happens in the early stages of any relationship, whether you are getting into it with a narcissist or with someone else. And this is exactly what the narcissist is hoping for when they start getting together with you.

As soon as you start to notice that your partner has flaws, which is going to come out at some point, it is going to improve a regular relationship. You start to know who the person really is, and you decide if you really love them for who they are. But for narcissists, when you find out their weaknesses and their flaws, it is like ripping their clothes off in public and then having them stand there wearing underwear for the whole world to see. As a result, the narcissist is going to start feeling depression, embarrassment, and shame.

One thing to note here is how a narcissist will often be the first to leave the relationship. Just when you have felt tired with the relationship, and like it isn't going anywhere, you will find that the narcissist is going to leave you first. This is often due to the fact that the narcissist is going to have a big fear of being abandoned. But they may be the one who decides to end that relationship because it allows them to feel like they are in control of the situation. But they still end up with the depression.

Losing the narcissistic supply

Narcissists are going to survive off other people in order to fulfill their narcissistic supply.

The emotional imbalance that occurs within this kind of person, such as the depression and the mood swings, are going to be linked to the fear of a loss of this supply. Whether they realize it or not, the narcissist is always worried that they won't be able to fill this need, that they won't be able to find others who are willing to give them the attention that they need. Even a small fluctuation in the amount of narcissistic supply can seem like a big deal, and it can end up with them having depression.

Once the narcissist starts to feel depressed, they may decide that it is time to socially withdraw from others. They don't want others to know about the depression because it can seem like a sign of weakness. But what this actually ends up doing is cutting the supply that they need down even more. This means that not only will the narcissist fall into a deep depression, but they will end up turning to their closest partner to get the attention and admiration that they need.

This can be a hard thing for that partner to work through. The narcissist, in an attempt to get the same amount of narcissistic supply from one person that they used to get out of many more, will start to become more belligerent towards their partner. And then the depression that comes with the narcissist will become a horrible and vicious spiral for themselves and for all of those around them.

Think about how alcoholics and drug addicts act. They are often going to have a lot of feelings of self-loathing. They know that they need the drink or the drug that they are addicted to and that they can't get by without it, but these addicts also hate that they are so dependent on this and that they don't have the right amount of strength in order to get away from the addiction.

It is believed by some that the narcissist is going to hate themselves because of their addiction to that narcissistic supply. Just as depression will come with the other forms of addiction, the addiction that the narcissist has to their narcissistic supply could cause them depression as well. When it shows up in the narcissist, it is going to be a form of depression that they don't like at all, and to others, they will act out with a lot of aggression and belligerence.

The lower this narcissistic supply becomes, the more depression the narcissist is going to feel. They need to have that steady supply of admiration from those around them. And if they had been used to getting it from a close partner for some time, it can definitely cause a level of depression in them when the partner finally decides that they have had enough and they want to leave.

Depression can be the result of criticism from someone who usually gives them only praise. People with NPD are going to hate criticism and will be sensitive, not only because it is going to upset the worldview that they have, the worldview of being perfect, but also because they may see that it could potentially become a total loss of their supply from that particular person. And the anxiety that they feel is going to lead the narcissist to feel depressed in the long run.

This is the interesting thing that can happen with the relationship. With normal and healthy relationships, the individual is going to feel sad because the relationship has ended. They spent a lot of time with that person, building memories, and building up life with them. Even if they were the ones who decided to break it off and move on, there can be a bit of depression because of the loss of the relationship.

But the narcissist is going to see this situation in a slightly different manner. They are not going to be concerned about losing the relationship because they lost the person, regardless of how long they were in that relationship. Instead, they are going to be upset because their narcissistic supply is gone. They aren't sure where they are going to get their admiration and attention from in the future, and this is what will lead to their depression.

At the most basic level here, depression can be a feeling of desperate and complete loneliness. Because the narcissist is going to lack empathy, they are going to lose their ability in order to connect with other people in their lives. Even with this lack of empathy, the narcissists are going to crave attention. Deep down though, they are going to be some of the loneliest people on earth, wanting empathy from others but unable to give it back to anyone else.

Chapter 5: How to Handle Your Interactions with a Narcissist

Now that we have spent some time in this guidebook talking about narcissism and all of the different parts that come with it, it is time to take a look at how you should handle any interactions that you have with the narcissist in your life. There are many different places where you may encounter a narcissist. They may be your parent, your sibling, your aunt or uncle, your partner, your child, and even someone you work with. And with the instances of narcissism being so high and, on the rise, lately, you will find that it is more and more likely that you will need to interact with someone who has NPD.

Whether you need to stick with pleasantries or a light chat in the office hall, or you need to have a more serious talk with the person, you will need to change the way that you interact with the person who is dealing with NPD. Often, when you are talking to a person like this, you will find that the conversation isn't always going to come out the way that you want, think, or expect because of the way that the narcissist is going to handle it all. But when you have a better understanding of what you are able to expect from the narcissist, and you are able to handle them better, you will find that you can handle any narcissist who shows up in your life.

How can I talk to someone who has NPD?

Normally, when you stop and have a discussion with another person, there is an expectation of the way that the other person is going to respond in general. But if they don't respond in the way that you were expecting, you may be visibly shocked by that. Often, the response that you are going to get from a narcissist is going to feel like a punch in the stomach because it takes you so off guard. It is very helpful to be prepared for these responses so that you are not taken off guard and can keep the conversation going.

When you talk to a narcissist, remember that it is best to never react with impatience, anger, or fear. There are some neutral responses that are the best to use in order to reduce the amount of intimidation or control that the narcissist is going to try and use on that conversation. For example, you may decide to keep your attitude curious or one of patience, and going with some responses or questions like "I'm not so clear about what that means. Can you please tell me more or clarify?"

On one hand, these questions allow you to put up the emotional boundary that is needed and helps you to not take the statements of the narcissist in a personal manner. You don't want to ever let them put you in the trap of feeling responsible or guilty, and you want to be able to maintain a bit of control over the situation. The narcissist is going to try and push back against any of the boundaries that you are trying to put up. But staying strong and keeping things pretty neutral rather than fighting back will make this much easier.

Now, there are going to be some times when you end up in a group situation with an individual who has NPD. You can still use the same kind of questions that we talked about above in order to make sure there is emotional space around you and to make the narcissist remain accountable for their statements. If you are at a loss for the types of questions and comments that you can make, whether you are alone with the narcissist or you are in a ground situation, practicing some of the following can make this easier:

- How did you come to that position or decision? What helped you to reach that position?
- What things did you consider before you made that decision?

  Can you help me out by making the intent of that statement clear?

In general, if you can, these pointers are going to help you to be deliberate and force the narcissist to come out with what they want. Sometimes, they are going to back off because they don't want to fall into a trap and look bad. And if they do come forward, they are going to have to give up their true positions, which makes it easier for you to walk away.

There are a lot of different things that you are able to do in order to engage with a narcissist, no matter how you know them. Some of these include:

1. Always listen to what they are saying carefully and think some thoughts that are pleasant. Even take the time to smile.
2. If the narcissist meets with you and sees you as a good source of support or a source of acknowledgment or recognition, then the communication is going to be easier to handle.
3. Try to add in some truthful recognitions and positive comments when you talk to the other person. You want to flatter them and make

them feel good about talking with you, while still making sure that you are the one who is in control of the situation at all times. Never make the mistake of being insincere in flattering them because they will be able to see right through this.

4. Keep in mind that the narcissist not only doesn't like challenges or frustrations in their life, but they can't also handle it.

5. The narcissist is going to refuse to treat you as an equal to them, no matter what. Instead, they are probably going to have some unreasonable expectations of you, simply because, in their own minds, they are entitled to this.

How can I stay strong and not let the narcissist manipulate me?

Many times, the person who has NPD is going to need to be in charge, to be the one who is right, and they always want to achieve their own agenda and goals. Because of this, it is their goal to work and manipulate the other person to help them reach these end goals. And since many narcissists are going to be very convincing and charming, it isn't too hard to see why the average person is going to get caught up in all of this and become manipulated.

It is important that you stay strong and hold your ground. If the narcissist is going to manipulate you, then this means that you are going to lose out In the long run because you won't have control over your life. The narcissist is not going to care how much they use you, as long as they are able to get what they want. There are three kinds of rules that you need to consider when you are trying to make sure that the narcissist doesn't manipulate you and these include:

1. Don't respond to any of their arguments. Instead, be a listener who is kind. If you find that they keep trying your patience and you are not able to just sit and listen, then find a way to leave the conversation.
2. Set a firm boundary with them, one that allows you to meet your own needs. You can warn the narcissist when they have pushed too far, and make it clear to them what is going to happen if they decide to infringe on this boundary.

3. If you find it necessary, leave the situation and find ways that you can take care of yourself with no guilt along the way.

Many times, someone who has NPD is going to try and take reality and twist and turn it so that none of the blame can be placed on them, and all of it is placed on you. They will often deny any fault at all, and you may be accused of being a liar, judgmental, unfair, or mean.

It is common for these narcissists to try and manipulate you if they think that you are criticizing them. First, they may start to feel anger and become defensive around you. Then they may make some demands that they expect you to meet. And if you fail or refuse to meet them, then they are going to be outraged at this. But if you decide to get angry with the narcissist in return, you may get to let out some of your feelings, but it doesn't provide you any protection from the manipulation in the future.

If you are in a close relationship with the narcissist, they could use finances in order to get you to act in a certain way. For example, the narcissist may decide to make you feel obligated to them or dependent on them through the finances. It is a good idea, especially at the beginning of the relationship, to have your own financial support so that you can never be manipulated by this.

The narcissist is going to be really good at getting under your skin. And there may be times when you have trouble dealing with the strong emotions or words of the narcissist. If this is true, it is a good idea to walk away and take a break. You can also work on developing a stronger self-confidence and self-esteem at the same time. Taking care of yourself and remembering that you do matter during this is going to be the best way that you can protect yourself from a narcissist.

Can I get what I want from a narcissist?

When it comes to a significant other who is a narcissist, you may be able to get away and not have to deal with them any longer. But when it is a sibling, a parent, a child, or even a partner you have kids with, it may be hard to break off from them completely.

And if you really love your job, but there is a narcissist who works there, you may not be able to escape from that either. This brings up the question, are you able to get what you want out of a narcissist or are you doomed to only ever do what they want?

If there is something that you would like to get out of the narcissist, whether it is them to help out with some chores or you would like to find a better way to deal with them, the biggest key is that you need to have a good understanding of how their mind works. When you know the way that this person is going to react and respond to you, then it becomes infinitely easier for you to know the right way to approach them.

First, always remember that the person who has NPD is going to want, need, and look for praise and admiration all of the time. The drive of the narcissist is going to be directed towards independence, influence, power, intelligence, or beauty. If you are able to figure out which one of these validation types that the narcissist likes the most, you can use it in some compliments to them. And once you give the compliment, make sure that they hear it before you proceed.

Basically, if you want to get something out of a narcissist, you need to show them how much they are able to benefit from it. Yes, they will need to do something small for you, but in the end, they are going to get something much more significant out of the deal. For example, let's say that you want to go to a movie, and you want the narcissist to agree to go with you. You know that this narcissist likes to talk about their superior intellect skills and that this is important to them. You may say something like, "The reviews all said this is not a film for the weak-minded; only the quickest minds will figure out the twists and turns" can get them to agree to go do what you want.

This all may seem a bit manipulative, but it is really what we do with all of the relationships. If we want to eat at a certain place with friends, we may use our influence to convince them. You just need to concentrate your efforts a bit more when it comes to the narcissist.

How to stop being victimized or abused by the narcissist

Always remember that there should never be a time when you have feelings that you deserve anything less than respect.

But because of some of the common behaviors that come with narcissism, it is possible that you could become a victim of abuse if you get into a relationship with a narcissist. Sometimes, this is mild verbal abuse, and sometimes, this goes a bit further and becomes physical abuse.

Being a victim of a circumstance or an incident should not make you feel ashamed. Always think about getting help if you end up in that situation, no matter how you got there.

It is common for the narcissist to be charming, and to know exactly what to say to get you to be with them, to listen to them, and to take them in. And they may be able to hold up that façade for some time. But eventually, their true selves will come out, and you will be the victim left in the crossfire.

Work relationships, living relationships, and all other relationships are going to end up with some personality clashes at time. After the clash is done though, most people will find some healthy ways to resolve them and move on. But when the clash happens with a narcissist, it is almost impossible to resolve the clash. The narcissist is going to fight to be right, no matter whether they are actually right or not, and it can happen that you will become abused in the process. Never let this abuse slide or let it control you. There should always be a zero tolerance policy in all relationships, but especially with a narcissist, when it comes to abuse.

So, how are you supposed to avoid being a victim when you end up in a relationship with a narcissist? This can be hard. They often find a way to let themselves into your life, and all of a sudden, you have twirled around and living with them. But, as the novelty wears off and you start to learn more about them and their ways, you are going to be sucked in and may become a victim in this relationship with a narcissist. Some of the things that you can do to try and avoid this in your relationship include:

1. When you are communicating with a narcissist, whether it is over an argument or just a normal conversation, be prepared that their perception is going to be completely different from yours. And often, the narcissist is not going to consider the perceptions that you have.

2. You should always have a good support system behind you, including counselors, friends, and family so that you can still have some control over your life.

3. Have a life of your own. Often, narcissists want to make sure that they are able to be in control. They want to make sure that all of your attention is just on them and on nothing else. You can make sure that have your own life including financial independence, activities, hobbies, and work if possible to avoid complete isolation through the narcissist.

4. When you do communicate with this person, remember that you shouldn't take things too personally.

5. Make sure that you set up some realistic boundaries and then share them with the narcissist. Be ready to enforce these boundaries because it is likely that the narcissist is going to try and fight them

6. If you run into troubles where the narcissist becomes too demanding, you can use some topics like "I'm sorry you feel that way" or "Can I have a little breather to think about that?" can help you to get a buffer and think through

decisions, rather than getting caught up in the moment.

The way that you interact with the narcissist is going to be quite a bit different compared to the way that you interact with others around you. They are not going to respond in the manner that you think they will, they will often demand things that are way unrealistic, and they may even become abusive if their actions are not checked, and if they are not given what they want. Being able to alter the way that you interact with a narcissist is going to make a big difference in whether you are able to maintain the control that you need over your own life.

Conclusion

Thank you for making it through to the end of *Narcissistic Personality Disorder.* Let's hope it was informative and able to provide you with all of the tools you need to achieve your goals whatever they may be.

The next step is to start using some of the tips and tricks that are found in this guidebook when it comes to working with a narcissist or even getting treatment for someone who is already suffering from this condition. Many of us have come across a narcissist at some point in our lives, but very few know how to actually deal with this kind of person. This guidebook is going to give you the information and the tools that you need in order to do this.

Inside this guidebook, you are going to learn everything that you need to know about narcissistic personality disorder, or NPD, how to recognize the signs and symptoms of someone who has this condition, and even some of the best treatment options that you can use to help someone who has gone through this issue. Treatment is possible, and narcissists can start to learn how to change their way of thinking and talking, but it is something that takes time and it won't happen overnight.

Dealing with a narcissist in your life is never an easy experience. They are able to get full control over their victim, and they don't want to let go because this is the way that they get the focus and the attention that they want. Understanding the why behind all of this and learning the steps that you can take to change it around will make a big difference. Make sure to check out this guidebook to show you the exact steps that are needed to make this happen.